But You're Wearing a Blue Shirt

the Color of the Sky

But You're Wearing a Blue Shirt

the Color of the Sky

Selected Poems
by
Lucille Broderson

NODIN PRESS

ISBN: 978-1-935666-06-6
Library of Congress Control Number: 2010913214

Design: John Toren
Cover photo: Linda Close Broderson

Nodin Press, LLC
530 North Third Street
Minneapolis, MN
55401

this is for Phil

CONTENTS

2

3

FOREWORD

She has the eye and she has the ear. Lucille Broderson is one of the most natural writers I have ever had the joy of working with—a poet of brilliant detail (she doesn't miss much), effortless free rhythms, heartbreaking disclosures, exceptional emotional directness. In fact, it's no secret that I think she's a marvel, my old friend, and I won't stand long between the reader and these poems.

Lucille is fully human, as we could all wish to be; she goes into difficult areas of thought and feeling and she isn't shy—or seems not to be—about sometimes painful revelations. Resonant in her distress and her joys, she's funny, too, sometimes wickedly so, and shrewd, and so frequently deeply touching. Yes, most certainly, a marvel.

Whether or not it is true that "the poet is born, not made," I have to believe Lucille was meant to do this, to go into these caves, excavate these wounds, and bring onto the page, over all these years, what she has discovered there. There's a fearlessness about her. Writing should be daring, and this poet has, at the age of ninety-four, kept her wild mind. Her poems occur to me, keep me company, through my imaginative life.

She weaves her themes, her obsessions, effortlessly, and like all good writers, she has confidence in her subject matter: the loss and presence-absence of her beloved Phil; the ache for a mother who sent her out "unfinished," who called and called "but we never heard"; her haunted sense of being "the last / of

all those faces around the table, / all those bodies warm in bed."
Her passion for nature, rooted in her Minnesota and Wisconsin
lakeshore life, goes deep and runs strong—so much, always, to
perceive and celebrate, so much to mourn.

And with so much to choose from, I'll end with the latter
lines of her poem "Heaven":

> Not another soul in sight, me alone
> behind the blower, humming over and over
> Rock of ages cleft for me
> though long ago I'd forgotten the words.
> And can you believe I felt
> my being here on this planet—
> blood pulsing, breathing coming,
> again and again in the midst
> of all this enormous universe
> (imagine!)—my being here
> actually mattered.

Reader, here she is.

— *Michael Dennis Browne*

1

EIGHT OF US

Brought Mother jars of crocuses,
stole the neighbor's watermelons,
forgot to hoe the corn.
Whirled our waists on the school's iron fence,
exposing our panties and petticoats.
Smashed our dolls, then howled
with the broken pieces in our hands.
Fought over the wishbone, wouldn't eat the neck.

Father shook the brothers,
rapped his knuckles on their heads.
Mother muttered and rubbed
our sunburned backs with vaseline.

We thought we'd last forever,
but we grew long and brittle
and split like fluff on dandelions.

Johnny left first, there was nothing here to hold him.
Then Mary dropped laughing in a parking lot.
How like her, that big booming woman.
But dishes were piled high in her kitchen sink,
the dogs unfed for days.
Then it was Liz, always up first in the morning,
finally too slow on a busy street.

The others wrinkled and shrank, sagged
in their chairs, afghans on their knees,
eyes huge behind thick lenses.

In pairs they left, two in one year,
two in the next.

Now I'm the last,
of all those faces around the table,
all those bodies warm in bed.

SOPHIE ON THE PLAYGROUND

Ribbons trail from our little straw hats,
patent leather shoes crack in the dust.
You shine the toes with vaseline and invite me
to skip with you around the schoolhouse.
You like my new dress with the double flounces
and ask if you can wear it once.
Oh, you can wear my dresses.
You can wear my panties too, my little bra
and all my nighties. Pin me on your lapel,
hang me from your window shade,
paint your brows with me, rouge your lips.
Yes, yes, you can wear my dress.

OUR MOTHER

Dove in shallow water,
never seeing the rocks.
She drifted in clouds, always singing,
slept through days,
hanging sheets on the line, smiling.

Our mother pushed and pulled, the gale
lashing her skirt, and dragged the cow
with the laid-back ears to the barn.
Evening after evening, she bent
over the Bible
and last week's little blue tracts
strewn on the dining room table.

On Sundays she curled her hair
with a curling iron, laced up her corset
and the polished shoes with the Cuban heels
and went off alone to the bus.

Our mother watched the moon
through closed curtains
and danced alone in the parlor.
Our mother sobbed in her sleep,
but we never heard, she called and called
in the night, but we never heard.

HOW CAN YOU EVER BE SURE

"that what you write is really any good at all?"
the young Merwin asked the older poet.
How can I be sure that Mama loved me,
Mama who always said I was no trouble ever,
one push and I was born, no time
even to protect the bed.
How can I be sure there were eight
of us once, all dropped over sixteen years
from a mother who never raised her voice,
from a mother who said she never wanted any of us.
How can I be sure about me, that I'm any good?
That Mama was good?
Mama whom I never saw shed a tear,
when the youngest brother inhaled monoxide
and two of the babies lived less than a day.
What is good? Is a rose any good?
Or ants in the driveway? Or that worn-out
Bible on the table? Who will decide? I
who never shed a tear when Mama died?

THE SCREENHOUSE

I sit alone in the screenhouse,
high above the lake,
the breeze soft
on the flesh of my arms.
The heavy hollow splintered box
that is my chest, heaving.

Oh, Mama, you never finished me.
One smooth touch of your hands,
a pressing here and there,
a molding here and there.
But you were tired
or didn't have the time
or didn't want to, maybe.
You sent me out unfinished.
I can understand.
But the finishing has been so hard
and I have tried so hard, and you
could have done it, couldn't you?
So easy?

Through a rent in the canvas cover,
the scented touch of the sun,
like a mother's hand on hand.
And my head drops, my shoulders slump.
Now only the lull of lapping water.

ALONE AT THE OLD CEMETERY

It hasn't changed,
the water tower's the same washed gray.
That outhouse with the three holes
still smells like an attic.
Thank you, I say, to no one.

The clover's sweet and warm.
It's been a long while
but I know where I'm going.
A little hollow
and a lilac bush.

And there they are, the father
I hardly knew, two sisters, a brother,
the mother who was never afraid
but whose pink hands in her casket
frightened me.

How easily I let them go,
I, always off to the side,
watching. To sit again
at that shabby table,
lift the blue and white creamer, say,

Say what? You weren't good enough?
You weren't what I wanted?
Yes, how easily I let them go.
How hard to leave them now.

I pause a moment at graves
of children who died before I was born.
Annie,   *Alas, she has left us.*
and Adam under a carved lamb, its nose eroded.

As I turn toward the gate, I see
by an old oak, Jean, Joan, the Woodward girls.
How I envied them, pretty and blonde,
with zipper overshoes, a live father
and a white muff.
Dead at twelve, drowned.
And I envy them still. I'll always envy them.

FACING IT

Arthur lifted his father's eyelids,
first one, then the other,
the eyes clean, clear.
No, Arthur, no.

He pressed his father's neck,
Getting hard, he said.
He knew
I didn't believe.

Everything slows, the light goes gold,
my cheeks glow, give off little rays,
my lips soft and thick
like melting wax.

Everything goes, the breathing very slow.
It stops and you aren't sure
and you listen and listen.
The cold moves up so slowly.

Arthur touched my shoulder.
They want to be told,
the people here, what I want done.
Of course.

I walk then to the elevator,
get off at the ramp,
get in the car,
drive up the streets.

They are there before me,
all those cars in the driveway.
And I see
the house needs paint.

NEEDLEPOINT PILLOW

Someone's given me birds,
stiff and frozen on cloth, but my birds
fly from maple to birch to white wooden fence.
My birds skip in the water, then out, foam on their feet.
They stand in puddles near a swamp,
let me stand there, too,
but never startle, never leave.

I shouldn't have left.
I should have watched them lift you from the pillow.
No, I should have removed the pillow,
laid your head on the bed. And I
should have straightened your legs, opened your fists,
placed your hands across your chest.
I should have drawn up the sheet
and kissed you again
before you were wheeled away.

OUR LAST VACATION

Strawberries bloomed in a wooden box

high on the deck that was ours
for one day only.
The day had gone too soon, cloudless first,
then a creeping overcast.
Finally, only the faintest sunset, a white sunset.

I wanted to keep the day, as I wanted
to keep the children, as I wanted
to keep you. Wrap the day
in wine-soaked cloth,
store it forever in some ancient cellar.

I could feel the sea rise and chill
around me. I went inside, found you
lying in the dark. How cool your lips.
I pulled an afghan over your shoulder,
gripped your hand through the wool.

MY HOUSE IS YOUR HOUSE

I want you to go back, I said,
to the earth you came from.
I'll scatter you from an airplane,
dig you in at the roots of a maple.
I'll let you out slowly behind the boat
as a daughter rows or over the side
of your canoe as a son paddles.

But I know now
my house is your house.

I've put you with the green glass float
I had no shelf for,
with the mobile of silver ships
I never hung,
beside the girl holding the red candle
that shone for years
in your mother's window.

You're in the TV room, near the chair
I always sit in, you're in the old walnut commode
with the hinged top, the one
your grandfather built and lined with tin.
You're in the place
for things that have no place.

A THOUSAND YEARS

King Arthur's dead
over a thousand years.
In a thousand years, I'll be dead
                              and you.

The stars will be here
and the moon. That satellite
that swept through the comet's tail
will long since
have burned to earth.

In the bedside drawer
he seldom used,
I found the papers: scraps,
twisted, torn.

He'd scrawled the words over and over,
I've lived a thousand years!
And under each scrawl, his name
again and again.

So he knew
when he turned to that wall
it was time to leave,
to find the seaweed
we yearn to be coiled in.

REQUIEM

The children tiptoe past my sleeping room,
past the chair I drowse in.
The days go like April's daffodils
and now the asters wither, too,
and I haven't even seen them.

I wait for the sound
of bluebells ringing.
An old pumphandle creaks,
water splashes,
tastes iron and runs cool on bare feet.

You move among the tall grasses,
wave a white handkerchief across the field.
I dreamed I'd see you in your old maroon sweater
but you're wearing a blue shirt
the color of the sky.

SOON THE GEESE WILL BE GONE

I sit here all day in this big chair
and listen to *Lohengrin* over and over,
watch the fire go out
and build it up, watch it
go out again and build it up.

Soon the geese will be gone,
as the years are gone, the children, too,
and the dogs and cats: Sam, who slept
on the bird feeder, Shell,
who wailed outside our bedroom window.

I have a good bed, a stove that doesn't smoke,
a full refrigerator. I write a check
the bank will honor.
I turn down the heat and no one tells me
it's cold. I have a phone wherever I sit.
No one asks who called Chicago? Burbank?

No one says, it's time to go to bed
or you slept late today or do you know,
your eyes spark when you make love.

HARVESTED FIELD

I walked in a moonless night
barely seeing the stubble around me . . .
I was looking for you.
You always said you'd meet me there.

Would you come if it were daylight
and everyone could say,
look, how faithful he is?
Would you come if the moon were shining
and you could see me, bright
as I was when we first met?

I sat on the old straw stack you plowed around,
hoping it would rot before the next planting.
I thought you'd be there with that old grin,
that you'd laugh, give me a little shove
and take me with you—wherever you've gone.

Although I heard the crackling behind me,
and knew your steps, you didn't come.

Now I walk the field in twilight,
the straw stack dank and crumbling.
Nettles sting and thistles cut my thighs.
In my throat an old crow nests.

THIS IS YOUR OLD AGE, LUCY

When the sky is too blue,
when robins come in flocks
and fight in the bird bath.
When chrysanthemums freeze in the sun,
and geese are fat and float on the lake.
When the children jump from the bus
and run to someone else's door.

When your teeth find white bread tough
and apples cut into your gums,
when your face puckers and is small in the mirror
and you smile at the nose
you are finally willing to own.
When the man in your life fondles your breasts,
whispers lovely, lovely, and you are off
high in the bleachers observing.

Time when it's time and you hear
the train whistle and wonder where it's been
all these years, when, after forty winters,
you visit your mother's grave and think of her there,
boxed in the ground beneath you, her pink hands
still folded over the crepe de chine dress.

And you know,
you don't have to pack your suitcase,
check airline times and tickets.
Now it's just the crow's call, the far-off
rumble of a plane. It's tiny
crystals rubbing, silk strings touching.

SEPTEMBER SUNDAY

I could follow the faithful
down the gold carpet,
pray before the pastor
with the always smiling face.
I could bow my head,
kneel on the little bench.

But I sit high on a porch,
birds scratch on the roof above me,
mallards swim by, swallows dip
from tree to tree. Ferns
are freckled with copper,
weeds yellow among the junipers.

I've done what I can,
picked berries in season,
cut back canes, snapped beans,
scrubbed down the mud-spattered walls.

I've buried the mother, the father,
the brothers, the sisters,
the husband.
The sick room is clean now,
the weeping over.

Let the day come, let it come
as dust billowing or hail
ripping leaves and baring trees.
Let the day be a black strip
on the horizon or a flash
of light across the valley.

YOU WATCH AND WAIT

Forgive me that I grew smaller
as I grew older, no greatness
in my walk, my dream.
Forgive me that I could not carry you
to that land of milk and honey,
that I could not show you the way.
The way, how I struggled to find it.
Here, there, beyond the bridge,
under the bridge, this side, that.
You watch me now. I see you
wanting, waiting.
You wait for another
to point the way ahead.
You wait for me
to let you take me by the hand.

LETTER NEVER SENT

This letter is about me, the real me, the mother
you've never met. The one you invite to dinner
on Christmas or Easter is an imposter.
Or perhaps you already know.
But you'll act surprised
and hug me hard when next we meet. "Oh, no,"
you'll say. "You're not like that."

I did not have a father, that's true. He died.
"Oh, how she loved him, how she misses him!"
But I never missed him. I found another . . .
in the Elsie Dinsmore book.
He meant business, that father.
No! No! Do this! Do that.
And I did it all. Right. How pleased Mother was.
A child that is no trouble.

I grew up not pretty but pretty enough
and a young man wanted me.
He was as good a father as the book father.
He found the house, paid the bills, ordered the children,
loved me, he said, but I never believed.
He died. Too soon, of course, but he left me
"well enough off": my home, my car, my bankbook.
But I never loved him. Nor the man who followed him.

Then I woke and knew I hated the world,
the people in it, the books that stood every which way

on my shelves, the pages I'd written,
the flowers on the table,
the wide snow-covered lake.

I never loved anything or anyone
but you, my children. Forgive me. It's true.

WILD GEESE

Once they led my car as it curved the lake,
their shadows long on the hood.
Once they appeared on shore without a sound,
slipped in the water as I swam by.
I moved toward them, not raising a ripple.
I didn't see them lift or skim out of sight:
one minute, the leader's black eye stared,
the next I was alone.

Now when I hear the wild geese cry,
I know I'll see them soar from some hidden bay,
turn and circle slowly over my head.
I'm like stone then, but as they swing away,
I laugh, and stretching tall as I can,
I call them back.

One day, they'll hover above me,
their white tails fanning
like a sigh as they settle around me,
the warm wings nudging.
And then, that urgent whisper.
Come, it's very late.

THE ART OF

I wanted a light song,
a funny song, one you'd chant
and hum to kids around the fire.

A sweet song you'd whisper
in a baby's ear.

I wanted a huge song,
a bellowing song
that would boom out to sea,
startling gulls and pelicans
and fish that sprint in the air.

I wanted a blue blue song
that would lull you off to sleep
and a orange-red streaked one
to wake you up again.

Most of all, I wanted
a slow dark song, a hidden forest stream,
deep and narrow, under vines
and overhanging moss and curling watercress,
a stream that finds
a rocky cleft and disappears,
winding through purple caverns
and porous yellow sand until it spills
again to quiet light
and flows forever on,
shallow, broad and clear.

WHAT I KNOW

Freedom is something I've never known.
The sky may know but the stars do not
nor the sun nor the moon or the tides or tornadoes
or babies growing in wombs.
Poor babes, they're on a track;
time will take them
inexorably on and on
and one day they'll see
there never was a choice for them
or the stars or the moon or me.
For here I am, a babe once, and think
all those years and years, eons, perhaps,
(how do I know?) I, proud ignorant fool, thought
I made the asides, the great leaps this way, that.
All the while I dreamed.
But now, at last, I see it all
and not through a glass darkly
but through a crystal clear as life,
clear as God, clear as whatever you'd like it to be,
Oh, I shall never dream again.
For now at last I am free. I see!

TODAY'S THE DAY

Today's the day I give madness away
and dance and dance and dance.

Trees' reflections green the lake.
What's under that slick is none of mine.
Up the way a chainsaw grunts and whines.
No messy limbs for that man.

A robin pecks at dandelions.
Hello, Bird, where are you?
In reincarnations, that is—
rungs and rungs above me and mine.
Whose fault is that?
Still.
Fun, is it? Worm yanking, stretching, snipping?
Any squeals?

Make me a rabbit next time round,
chomping tulips and lettuce leaves
and hiding young in window wells.

It's all yours, kids.
I pass it all along.
You read the papers, watch the tube,
pay the taxes, kill the brothers.
You burn the babies and black the globe.

It's all yours.

Today's the day I give madness away
and dance and dance and dance.

LATE AFTERNOON ON THE SHORES OF LAKE SUPERIOR

Another year and the leaves fall,
not the glorious reds but a drab yellow.
The lake so quiet today,
I could walk on it, see down
to the rocks below.
I can almost feel the gritty stone.
Near the shoreline, the boulders
that seemed such a bulwark
crack and splinter.
It's getting late . . . too late.
Soon, too, the doors will close.
I'll knock and knock but no one will hear.
Soon the child I was will come running
wanting to leap into my arms.
Soon, too soon, the night, then winter,
then the darkest of all darks,
but then the morning, the long long morning,
the morning never promised,
the morning that will never end.

LAST LOOK

Everything swells, mounds round in the grass,
trees shoot to the clouds.
Walks appear, small people parade in Sunday fashions.
I'm so far above, I have to bend
like a child gauging the hopscotch square.

You down there, I'm leaving.
I love your place with its sprouted seeds
and dandelions, bursting pods
and old women on steps, kerchiefs in their laps
bulging with peas to shell or beans to snap.

But I'm leaving anyway. The dogs howl in the night,
owls hoot, babies cry. My feet hurt,
my apron strings are in a knot I can't untie.
I wriggle out of the apron,
leave it standing there
ready for the next one.

Now my heart balloons. It needs
a bigger space. You know the place,
it's what you've always longed for
since you slung along in mother,
every movement wrapped.

2

UNCLE TED AT EIGHTY-FIVE

At night they came, through holes in the floor,
his wife and his son. How did they do it, the holes so small!
His brow wrinkled, his eyes still blue.
He asked me. *I* should know.

They crawled through holes by the TV,
slept in his bed. No room in the narrow cot.
They pushed at his back, pushed him out,
the floor cold to his sore feet. Why?

He'd given up wanting them, missing them.
Perhaps he never missed them, the always ailing wife
and the son who grew up but never left.
They'd all grown old together.
Now the wife and the son were dead.

Buried, too, he said. You saw. They can't
want the money. You've got it.

No, no! I said, the bank has your money. Remember?

He'd hauled me into his attic,
searched the rafters for glued-on envelopes,
uncovered the iron pipe with the concrete plug.
Inside bills, some saved for over fifty years.
Up there under the eaves, safer than banks.

Dig a hole in your yard, he said.
But I drove him to the bank, the box on his knees,

and in a room with a long table,
sat with a teller and counted.

They must want the money, he said. They saved it.
His wife from her brother's pension, the son
from janitor's wages. A whole drawer-full of crumpled bills,
gathered and crammed once a year into that iron pipe.

You give them the money, he said.
You tell them to leave me alone.

SINCE I BEGAN

burning, the green has vanished.
Only dull black ashes now. The wild roses
became rosebuds, then split into seeds,
grew green again, then pink. This over and over.
I cannot count the times.

Since I began, the father died
one clear cold night, the whole house shaken
hoarse with his breathing. And the mother,
that big warm woman, the tangle of tubes removed,
suddenly small and still.

The dogs grew old and crawled under the henhouse
or dropped near the stairway already rotting in the ravine.
The teasing brother who turned our sled runners
in the red coals of the furnace, who built the shack
where the snow-covered grass met the plowed field,
drove off one day in his truck, laughing, waving

and parked under an old cottonwood, ran a hose
from the exhaust to the cab, lay down
on the seat and never got up. And the little sister
who pounded on my bedroom door demanding her turn
at the Sunday funnies wandered off at the last,
a child, with another child on her shoulder.

And I looked down at the pen in my hand and the books
under my arm, shook my head and went on my way.
The trees are stark now and gray. One after another

they fall. The water flows less and less
until, finally, only stones and dust. But the roses:
they rise unasked for, sit in chairs and will not leave.

THE LAKE GOES QUIET AND GRAY

The geese, sixty at least,
are easy in the calm water.
They gather now, more of them every day.
Soon they'll lift their white bottoms
and long black necks and be gone,
the lake ice on the edge.

The water will darken
as the north wind streaks
across the surface.
Then the lake will firm over,
go quiet and gray.

This house is big enough for a brood,
but the brood is gone. Still how comfortable
this room, how comfortable in clothes,
how comfortable in bed.

The young watch, are amazed when you move,
no crutch, no bent back. They like steps
firm, eyes clear. Would take your arm,
then expect you to stop
and motion them on ahead,
want you to say softly:

It's okay, it's all right,
want you to say you don't mind
stepping back from the wide windows
and out of the room where the old clock ticks,
that you don't mind veering off
to those endless fields of ice.

JUST WHEN WE THINK WE'RE FORSAKEN

We feel the mist on our hair, smell
the snow-covered hills of our childhood,
the dikes we built and re-built
on that ever-dissolving beach.

Such a distant lost song.
We follow the sound through rain and sun
hunting the flowers we laid
on the graves of the mother, the father,
the pale phlox, the yellow chrysanthemum.

And we long to be slim again,
bones with little flesh,
just the wire of us
leaning into the wind.

AT SEVENTY-EIGHT

I hear in myself the lapping of water
                              —Czeslaw Milosz

But I do not hear, I yearn to hear,
the lapping of water near the boathouse.
No longer to dream of death: sinking slowly, quietly.
There's no end to the clouds in the distance,
racing toward me over the water,
painting the water black. No end
to the lightning, here! There! Here! Here!

Oh, fathers, why can't time move another way,
off through the fields, the snow-filled fields.

One hour comfortable, knowing the answers,
nothing to fear, each step easier and easier,
then the nagging way back in the brain.
The "watch it" and then
MY GOD, WATCH IT!
The roadblock, the great spiked logs in the road.

Somewhere a placid pool, a stand of ancient pines,
needles feet-thick under the heavy branches.
Somewhere a stream descends
in hundreds of tiny waterfalls.

This morning, fog, dew on the windshield,
the windows. The lake an abyss,
the unknown, the unknowable.
Later, the sun, the lake wide open,
the red jagged rocks on the bottom

clearly visible and hardly a ripple.
At dusk the fog comes back.
Somewhere a child swings in the twilight.

Somewhere a child climbs library steps, stands small,
expectant by the librarian's desk.
Shelves and shelves of books. Banks of high windows,
sturdy little chairs in a half-circle.
Barely heard, a dog barks.
One lives on and on and there is no peace.
It's time, I say, to board up the windows
bolt the doors, drown the kittens
and feed the mice to the snake.
Time to haul off the rancid corn,
the dead cow and decaying horse,
to find the river and float away.

Live! snaps a crow from high in the cottonwood.
Live, for Christ's sake!
Wake! Wake!

And I do wake—from a long sleep
and know I've grown softer, that the earth
is not as hard as it was.
Today in these quiet woods, the sun shines,
clouds off over the lake,
clouds to every side
but here, the sun and the blue sky.

Somewhere, a mother at the dining room table,
books, papers, sprawled everywhere: Sunday's lesson.
A child sits on the floor and waits.

AND THEN THE RAINS CAME

I'm scared, I told the children.
They're old now but still my children. Responsible, too.
You didn't call, I said.
>The phone was dead.
Oh, no, not all the phones. Jeanie, John, too, has a cell phone.
>Not at the graveside
But you wouldn't be burying anyone. Who died?
No one spoke. And then the rains came
and once the shower was over there wasn't a soul around.
Where did you all go? I yelled.
>Shhh . . . you'll wake her.
Who?
>*Oh, you poor thing, come here you poor wet thing.*
I'm not your dog, I said and anywhere—where are you?
>We're here, Ma. Right here!
It was then I began to wonder.

IN THE END

All that last day at the cabin,
the lawnmower held you up, you
who could barely stand.
You rammed and rammed the mower
into the raspberry thicket
until we had lawn
where we didn't need it,
didn't want it.

That night, holding your night pail,
your hand went limp. The warm yellow
flowed onto the pine floor, between the planks.
Your teeth clenched. You wailed, a high keening wail.

Once the sounds that came from your lips
were words. When you'd nick a finger
or bump a shin, you'd glare at me, say,
I'd better not get really sick,
you'd never be there.
Then the cancer grew in your brain
and each day you became less and less,
and I was there. Surprised, but I was there.

You were my little boy then, feet wide apart,
rolling around the house in a toddler's gait
How I loved nuzzling your neck,
squeezing your shoulders. For days
I lay in your arms, sobbing.
You held me tight, your eyes wide,
no change at all on your face.

AFTER

The eaves sag on the house,
the dog grays,
its eyes film over,
there are lumps on its legs.
It doesn't get you up in the morning.

Even your daughter's love
for you, her Daddy, goes.
You die and she looks at her mother
for the first time.

You leave and your clothes
hang untouched for a year.
On a hanger, a suitcoat with a shirt under it,
a tie folded in at the neck.
Your wife leans against it, crying.

Now your son wears it,
feels comfortable, he says.
He's seen your bankbook, knows
how much money you left.

Your wife raises her face
to another man, wants more from him
than he can ever give.

OUR ANCESTORS WANT US TO BE HAPPY, HER SON SAID

"I'm going to miss you," he said.

"But I'll always be with you, remember?
Look at your hands. You'll see."

And he sat down next to her.
"Are my hands like yours?"

They were. Such power in his.
How frail hers, all wrinkled and shiny.

★

"Can I see the ashes?" he asked.

"But they're in a box, wrapped." Still
she went to the chest, lifted the neat black box.
"How heavy it is. I'd forgotten."

He took his pocketknife and pried up the lid.
Inside the clear plastic sack, the gray ashes.
Like oatmeal, he said, and unwound the fastener,
reached in his hand, touched what was left of his father.

★

"Let me hold you again," he said.
"Tell me—what do you think of death?"
"I think death is beautiful," and then quickly,

"Now where did that come from?" and she laughed.

★

"Could I have a little? Some of our ancestors
drank their fathers' ashes. In a little tea, maybe?"

"With lemon?"

"Just plain tea," and he reached above her
into the cupboard, brought down
a small teapot and a thin china cup.
"Oh, good," she said, "your father hated drinking tea
from a mug."

★

In the other room the box . . . waiting.
"I don't think I will," he said at last.

"Yes," she said, "I know."

"Someday—when the others are here,
when we're all together."

"Yes," she said. "I know."

TANTE ANNA SPEAKS

Such a quiet place, lots of space
and the moon, always a new moon,
all of it calm as a still-life,
as an oak in an acorn,
as I was once and she was, too.

And then:
tired of it all, she says,
bring me a hot water bottle and a book,
any book. Not to read;
it's to hold the window up,
the sash is broken, don't I know?

I never know, I say,
and why didn't you ask the man to fix it,
the man in the moon,
the one you're mad about, mad at, mad over.

I'm tired of this, she says,
bring me a tree, the one that grows in the basement.
Better still, the one that's under the sea.
You can find it, you put it there.

And so we're off again, bellowing
and screaming as we always do.
Years of it now. She's tired of it all,
she says again.
It all? I say. What's "it all"?
And now she spits out the window,

yells at me. "I'm happy, see, see?
I hit him . . . hit the sun."

The light fails as it always does,
and the sounds . . . oh, the wails, the tears.
Oh, Lord, forgive me. I have no one, no one.

Was that her cry . . . or mine?

THE BIRTHDAY GIRL

Planes rumble, clouds dark in the west.
A lawnmower hums and the birthday candles grow
from one to fifty to too many to count.
The cake, dried to a crust,
stands on the basement bar
though the smell of mold is everywhere.
But who, now, is there to care?
Surely not the birthday girl
as she begins to relax, then
slides slowly over the cliff.
No hurry, no waste, no loss.
Somehow the others don't seem to see.
They go on joking around the barbecue,
complain that the chicken's burned,
but "Aw, shucks, who cares?"
And another cork is popped,
another can tossed to the trash.

BEWARE

Never jump into this, I said. Important always to check your
gray purse, then ask the horse if he's ready. Don't wait for the
sheets to dry. What matter the dog's mistakes? What counts
is the table and the little boy. Not the chair, never concern
yourself with the chair. Chairs are for sitting, it's true; for
ruminating in, dreaming perhaps. They aren't to build highways
or tunnels under the sea. No, forget the chair, even when its
pull is strong enough to make a parrot screech. Desist, stop,
cease. Be a little girl again looking for your voice or your old
doll dishes wrapped and clinking in the gray blanket. Beware
of tables, of little boys, of mistakes. Beware of roses in crystal
and little boys screeching love. No, never jump on the table or
into the purse. A mouse will find you there, attack you with
tweezers. No end to the pain, the sorrow. A mother weeping, a
child lost. The clouds nowhere, only the sun too bright in the
sky. No, watch for the pen. It can spill things you never knew
you owned. It can turn that gray purse into a cow's ear. It can
turn you into a red-headed witch with a hare-lip and one leg
missing. It can make you into what you think you are: a demon
screeching from the other side of the moon, a lady mounted
on an ass, sheets for her dress, a doll grown old and weary, mud
in its eyes. Beware of boys searching for voices especially the
boy with the gray beard and rheumy eyes, the one who shouts
"Hallelujah" from the sandbox and asks for a light for his cigar.

WEBS

The flowering almond is now very full
not knowing that in a few months
it will be bare twigs covered with snow.
I didn't know either that time would come.
The old stuff: roses fade, grass turns brown, leaves fall.
Today hundreds of dew-covered webs
shining among the tamaracks and beyond them
the great lake, the frightening, inviting lake.
And all of it whispers, Come!
And I whisper back, Yes, yes. One gets tired
and time draws out . . . thin as taffy
pulled the length of the room,
taffy they pulled, remember? Who? When?

THE SMALL BOX

There's no running now to Mother
or handing this to you,
here, you take it, you can handle it.
There's no way to waken,
shake off the dream,
settle again to the pillow.

Winter comes on in a blue haze,
creeps under the door
and around the shutters.
I close my eyes
see blossoms thick on the tree.
But the tree sheds in a downpour
and only twigs remain.

They've given you back to me
in a small box.
Now I check the locks at night,
put shovel and sand in the car.
Another man smiles and places
the star on my Christmas tree.

VISITORS

I'm exhausted, I said.
I'm tired to death, I said.

But you spoke and I rose
lithe and young and ready.

You spoke
and birds flew in my window,
even a red-capped sparrow
fluttered about the room,

then left.

Why do you leave? I said,
Come back! Come back!

But the birds were gone,
had never
been there, you said.

You spoke

but you too were gone,
had never been there,

you said.

WHAT HAUNTS ME

How to walk
to the edge and never quaver.
How to stop
for one quick glance over the shoulder,
one small wave. How to be haunted
and stand relaxed, not giving a sign
to the dogs by the side of the road.
Looking them straight in the eye.
Hush, you dogs, hush!

WE STOP TO WATCH THE HANG GLIDERS

Too many words in the language.
How to get back to *see, come, go.*
No end to the wrangling.
Bombs in the night,
children blasted, their eyes and limbs gone,
old women sprawled in the streets.

On the mountain top, the man strapped
to the hang glider sprints off the rock,
spreads flat on his belly. Now he soars
over the valley. His wife follows, laughing.
She sinks beneath her husband,
finds another valley, slides from sight.

My man, watching with me, laughs, too.
He also tires of words. Jumping from the car
he runs to the highest rock, sways over the cliff,
shouts, Now me! Now me!

I grab for his shirt tail.
Not yet! Not yet!

SNOWSTORM

Snow in your head,
a blinding raging snowstorm,
specks of blood in the snow.
They found the little boy
outside in the snowbank,
his clothes torn off . . .
by his best friend, the mongrel pup.
The dog didn't bite him.
Just his clothes in the dog's stomach,
snow between the little boy's toes.

All wrong, snowstorms in the brain.
Let's have a river there instead,
a quiet cool river hardly moving.
Let's have a dog
swimming along with his master,
looking back, watching, guarding.
Let's have it right, shall we?
A picnic on the bank, frisbees flying.

ROSES

Of course I am sick,
tired of the way I turn
toward the madhouse
instead of the church.
The devil beckons,
garlands around his hooves.
I rushed this running away from you,
O my handsome one,
and then, my dying one.

And all the while
you were becoming roses
crushed in a pink dish.

WHITE MILK AT DAYBREAK

(after Paul Celan)

We wake on the hour of dread,
pray to the one who holds us, who carries us on her hip,
who could drop us over the void or lift us among the stars.
We pray and pray and feel within the worms
begin to crawl, the mold begin to form.
The cold, oh, the cold.
We creep beyond the haystack, dig deep in the fertile loam,
down down we sink, our home, our home.
We bow our heads before the plow,
whisper, "cover us, cover us," over and over,
until all around, the meadowlarks, the daisies, the clover,
until all around, the praises rise from the sea,
from the lakes, from the rivers, from the mountains,
the valleys, the plains. All around the notes
rise and rise and suddenly the clouds disperse.
The sun! Oh, white milk of the sun!

3

IN AN OAK TREE'S HOLLOW

Oh, yes, there's an angel.
Don't ask to see.
Don't ask to hear.
Don't ask to feel the wing.
The way is there.
You've forgotten it.
Perhaps tomorrow
when swallows dip over waters
in early morning, perhaps
when you open your eyes,
turn to the wall and stretch.
Perhaps at that moment, not too bright,
sun through leaves, birds singing.
If not then, in early evening,
the stars coming out, a dark patch
on the horizon, a blue-black patch.

You'll remember.

ON THE SHORES OF LAKE SUPERIOR

It won't last, this place.
First the wide red rocks will go.
Then the ledge-hugging fir and birch
will lean little by little over the lake
until they upturn, roots in air,
their branches whipped clean and bald
with endless washing.

I rock in the swing we hung
between two maples our first summer here.
Slats are rough and twisted, the chain
corrodes, the air is so clear
I see shadows on the far shore.
All around the aspen twirl their yellow leaves.

Over the meadow behind me,
I hear the already changing voices
of my grandsons gathering wood.
And a few feet away, the bank crumbles . . .
exposing the roots of our oldest pine.

You drop a hand on my shoulder,
and give the swing a gentle shove.

AFTER MANY DAYS

The child, relieved to be old,
sits under a skylight in the only chair on the big porch,
released from the clamor of babies and the young,
released from the quarrels, the ugliness
of a world she doubts will ever be healed.

He was tired, her husband had said years before,
and now she knows how tired he'd been.
Is there a time when what seemed important
is like an ant on the porch floor,
when what one wanted is only a shadow almost forgotten?

Is there a time
when being tired wears a smile
and holds out a welcoming hand?

BROTHER

The day comes when he can no longer speak
though he tries
and the hospital calls
but I will not hear.
All that day they call.
I leave the house with the ringing phone,
turn from the waiting phones
on the streets and in corridors,
call in, at last, the day gone.

Come, they say, and I go.
There, all in order, quiet, clean,
water pitcher on the table,
the white sheets, the gown
with ties in back. On his side
still alive, knees curled to his chest,
my brother. He and I the last of eight.

"You can leave now, Harry,"
a nun's cool voice,
"your sister is here."

Has he really waited for me?
I hold his hand, see it go blue
and I think of the car he built at seventeen
Ah, those careening rides on the gravel!
He tortured me in that old jalopy,
always that red handkerchief around his head.
But, oh, Harry, happy Harry,
how I loved you then.

Can he hear? Can he see?
You're a good man I tell him,
and I know you're bitter, you've a right
to be bitter: all those years
a father to the rest of us.
And who among us ever said thanks?

At the doorway, a young woman, eyes soft,
wants to pray with me.
I shake my head, squeeze his hand,
lean closer. Mother said
prayers are private, remember?
Mother was never afraid, remember?

I am at home there, even when the gurgle starts
and the brown liquid rises from his mouth
and flows down over the white beard,
onto the neck and under the gown.

Then it is over.
I wait, for a long while, I wait.

At last, I release his hand, raise the bed rail,
hesitate, then touch a tissue to his lips,
bend down to kiss his forehead.

NOW THAT YOU'RE ALONE

Should you be sad when the brother goes
and you are then, at last, the last?
There are so many waiting, pushing you.
The river moves too fast. Fish swim
against the current, hold up fins
to keep the water back.

There will be days that leave
before they've started, days that start
at dusk and never brighten,
nights that crawl in unnoticed
and never leave at all.

But there will be smiles broad
across the whole horizon, lips that purse
and whistle softly, never once releasing
their siren pull. There will be laughter then,
and what a joke it was and how'd you think
it would be and ain't it great
we cannot let them know.

THE LITTLE GIRL WHO WANTED HER PICTURE TOOK

(the past)

From those two on the porch steps,
his peck on her cheek, her seething chest,
the past began.

Chickens in a dusty yard,
a cow in a broken-down barn.
Fields blue with crocuses.
Little boys with empty perfume bottles
and daisies from their mothers' old straw hats.
Homage to the princess,
the giggling, unsuspecting one.

Time, though, goes: the father dead in the parlor,
the mother, her faded dress worn thin at the belly,
moves silently about the old house.
The little girl, pudgy now, red-faced, pimpled.

Mama, where are you? How do I say "hello"?
Where does the fork go? The spoon?
Mama, help me, there's a cloud, a black cloud!
But Mama's off where she's always been,
floating in hymns and the infinite.

Then: out of nowhere, the suitor, the husband.
"You're actually pretty," a sister says.
Ah, yes, the acne gone, the waistline trim.
And . . . oh, the smile!
But the man has a great cloud, too, and a need

to scream and fling the doors wide.
And there are the babies and rugs and beds and floors
and water: dishwater, washwater, bathwater.

Tell me, is this it?
Yes, my dear, this is it!
Mama, is that you speaking? Mama?

Then: *this* is no longer *it*.
Gone, the father, the mother, the sisters, the brothers,
the husband.
Gone, too, the babies, tall men now with graying hair,
hallooing faintly, intermittently
from the tops of mountains or across the seas.
Even the daughter who clung to her hand
now waves from a plane, "Bye, Mom, Bye."

RUBBLE BESIDE A CANADIAN ROAD

Once the mountain fell,
hundreds of tons of rock,
huge slabs and tiny pebbles,
all at once a roar,
a slipping, a covering,
and all the houses were gone.

And all the children,
all the chickens and cows
and cats and dogs,
all the mothers and fathers
and chairs in the kitchen,
swings on the lawn,
all the pickles in jars,
and jam smeared on buns.
Bibles in parlor tables,
underwear in drawers
and little drawstring pouches
filled with silver.

Trees moved in the night,
backed away softly over the cliff.

I stop the car,
hunt for the mounded cone
of an anthill, a wasp nest
under the steps. No cone. No nest.
No caterpillars on an alder bush.
No bush. No one.

Wherever I look
I keep seeing my face
gray without features.

ALTHOUGH I AM SAD TONIGHT

I will not sing of darkness endlessly weaving,
I will sing of long rolling waves I see from the cabin porch,
of ferns under the balsam and red and yellow flowers
that as evening approaches
draw their petals tightly upward.
I will sing of the lumbering rump of a bear
as he disappeared today around the outhouse,
of the newborn fawn a doe
left for a moment in my driveway.
But tonight the wind whirls and sings as I cannot sing
and the wide lake and the wide sky
become one deep luminous blue.
And every tree limb, trunk and leaf is marvelously black.
Now there's nothing to do but sit . . . absolutely still
as the color deepens until at last there is nothing.

ONE DAY YOU WAKE

How cold you are,
how stiff your fingers.
All you want is a warm hand
to hold, and familiar feet
in the hallway.

You thought it would be different,
but here you are
like others you've known:
tubes in your nostrils,
a sour odor on the sheets,
your already-aging children
turning away.

Now a nurse hovers,
begs you to swallow the pill,
motions at the cup on her tray.
No, no, enough is enough.

One can let the flowers go,
the meadows, too, and the bells.

SOMEWHERE TO GET TO

But where? the map is never there, lost perhaps,
never drawn maybe. For sure you do not have it.
No directions on a square of paper . . .
turn left at the corner, watch for three pines on the right.
No scribbles on a card. But now and then the shout:
This way! No, not there! Here! No, no. You dummy!
So on you go, to somewhere,
and you lose your face, your shape.
You're with all the other shapes and faces.
How comfortable
to see yourself in every face, every shape.
How easy to smile now, to sing.
How easy to be no one on your way to nowhere.

SUNBROWNED TOES

Climbing on the haystack,
squealing up the lookout tower,
giggling over Sam or Jerry or John.
He likes you. No! Not him, not him!
But Acey! Acey Turner.

Two little girls by the side of the road,
sunbrowned toes wiggling in the dust.
Now the big old wagon and the dirty white horses
with the wide wide hooves.
And high in front on the springy bench . . . Acey
on his trip to the gravel pit.
Acey's grin, Acey's holler.

Oh, Acey Turner, where did you go?
And that torn blanket under the cottonwood:
two little girls drinking sour grass tea,
the tangy taste of the brittle stems, the yellow flowers.

RENDEZVOUS

I danced alone today, swirled,
swung, and all the time he was there,
smiling, waiting to catch me, hold me.
I'd forgotten how tall he was,
but my arms knew and rose to meet his.
I could feel his chest,
those swells under the smooth shirt.

By the big windows, I danced
and watched the ducks dip and play on the lake.
I reached out to them, too, pulling,
pulling them toward me. They
flew right at me, swerved and disappeared.

I dream too much of his leanness,
the warm body I slept against.
The other man will soon be back,
a round little man, hardly taller than I am.
But I'll run to meet him, hold him.
It's his heart I'll be listening for,
it's the sound of his breath.

WINTER, AND YOU AND I AND THE UNIVERSE

Pondering today the imponderables:
me, you, my soul, my existence, yours:
all buttons in a glass jar, meaningless
as tears from a willow in the morning dew.
And so pondering the imponderables, I sit,
a pain in my thumb as I grip my pen, snow
plopping in great gobs off my roof as a man
shovels above me. Why is he up there
and me here by the fire and with books
around me? Why do his hands shake at forty,
mine steady at twice his age? Why the earth,
the sky? The universe?
So it is on the dreary day I ponder
the imponderables and feel myself go blue
with exhaustion and sensibly, wisely,
I quit!

BY THE BIG LAKE

The arm of the swing is cracked and gray,
I'd forgotten.
Another year and the leaves fall,
one by one now, not the glorious
reds of the maple but a drab yellow.

The lake so quiet today, I could walk on it,
gaze down at the red rocks below.
How near that huge skewed rectangle
is to the surface. I can almost feel the gritty stone.

The bank erodes and near the shoreline
the rocks that seemed such a bulwark
crashed and splintered, only rubble now.

It's getting late, too late.
Soon the doors will close.
I'll knock and knock
but no one will hear.

Soon the child I was
will come running and leap into my arms.
But we've already done this, I'll have to say,
but thank you, sweetie, thank you!

THE PHONE CALL

I answer, though I swallow hard.

Oh, hi! I say.
How'd your day go? How's yoga,
how's the tai chi, the walk in the park?
Is your wrist better?
Better, she says, not *much* better.

I look at the clock. How long?
An hour? Two hours? Me, a metronome.
Oh?   That's too bad.   That's good.
Over and over, but tonight the long pause.
I'm afraid, she says, and I catch my breath.
Not the devil again? But I say nothing.
I have this terrible fear she says.
What will I do? When you're gone,
when you die?
Oh, I say, suddenly alive and strong. You'll be fine!
I was sure I couldn't function without your father.
And I've been fine!
The cats aren't good, she says.
They won't eat this new food.
Try another brand, I say.
I can't afford another brand, she says.
Well, get another brand, I say. I'll pay.
Remember I didn't ask you to, she says.
Yes, I know, I say. But I want to.
Your cats are important. Important to me, too.
I won't be calling so often anymore, she says.

It's too much for you. I've been dumping on you.
No, no, I say. Everyone needs someone to talk to.
Well, I guess that's all I have to say, she says.
And then . . . Oh, I forgot . . . I've been dating again,
an older man. He's awfully nice. He reminds me of Dad.

Oh? I say, that's . . .
But she's already left the line.

THE CABIN AFTER THE REUNION

The new needles on the balsam are full
and heavy with rain.
No more thunder but very dark.
No fire in the stove, no wood in the woodbox.
The door to the room with the unmade bed closed.

Age, do things the easy way, the fast way
or don't do them at all.
It rains harder now:
heavy plops on the chimney pipe.

Yesterday, her sons at the cabin, their voices low,
then loud, then louder,
the sudden silence, the apologies, the hugs.
"They opened an old wound!" the second son cries
and rushes outside to crumple at the cliff's edge.
The little boy who ran to her so long ago
here, fifty years later, this quivering handsome man
and the sobs that will not stop. "An old wound."
"My little boy," she murmurs over and over,
lips on the white head.

Her wonderful sons, people after all, just people.
One day, joy; the next, a foot in the trap,
the gnawing at the metal, then at the flesh.
As each moves forward, she moves forward,
as each drops, she drops.

Take Nortriptiline, the young psychiatrist told her . . .

The doctor was dressed in white,
not a simple tailored dress
but all pleats and lace and ties and belts
and on her feet the tiny heart-shaped shoes.
"No, no," the mother responded and shook her head.

The rain lighter now.
Occasionally, the porch chimes; deep and varied tones
and near the lakeside windows,
a balsam fir grows tight to an aspen,
its branches hug the older, dying trunk.

HEAVEN

Can you believe . . . the snow,
how it glows this morning,
I sang as I got the blower
and cleared the driveway.
The evergreens, oh, how dazzling, too,
their boughs bent to the ground.
Sun glinting everywhere, even in ruts
in the unplowed street.
Not another soul in sight, me alone
behind the blower, humming over and over
Rock of ages cleft for me
though long ago I'd forgotten the words.
And can you believe I felt
my being here on this planet—
blood pulsing, breath coming,
again and again in the midst
of all this enormous universe
(imagine!) my being here
actually mattered.

RELAX

Relax. You've had enough trying.
Aren't you ready to weep at the waste?
You made it over that rickety bridge, it's gone now.
Good you got here at all. Oh, *profound,* is it?
That's what you'd love to be . . . just plain wise.
Plain? Now the lips sneer, the head shakes.
God, woman. Give in! But you, so serious,
can't or won't listen. Well, one can always find
a reason to slump away discouraged. But you're
the tough one, the strong one. A prayer perhaps?
A book? Shaw, Russell . . . de Sade? Now you're daft!
Yes, laugh! Love it, love all the words, you lucky one.
You still can read, still can hear, with aids, of course,
still can ponder, wonder, curse. Yes, curse the language.
But what a gift! See—there on the TV, his words careful,
slow, his face somber, a terrible sadness in him,
that black leader of the fractured country. So much
depends on him—so little on you. Relax.

HOME LATE, THE LAMP LOW

"A man who died with grace,"
the surgeon said
when I ran into him months
after Phil was gone.
Closure, I told my friends. Things
must be tied in knots, tight, the pillow cover,
the opening stitched: tiny stitches, overlapping.

Yesterday, the stranger,
sprawled on the floor of the supermarket.
The brown overcoat, the polished shoes,
his face flat against the cold tile.
I longed to bend down, to touch, but I pushed
through the crowd and wailed all the way home.
It makes no sense, I said over and over.
I never cried like this for any of them,
now too many of them.

Last night, roiling smoke
filled the whole fireplace
and I sat there shivering, damp and cold.
The smoke cleared finally,
leaving behind a space so dark.

We didn't know
playing back then in the dirt and dandelions
that I'd be the one to end up alone,
home late, the lamp low.

This morning, the crows came, dozens circled.
They could have been blackbirds
flocking for winter but they were crows
and crows never leave.

Yet the day brightens ... now the sun
and the grass suddenly greener than summer;
all the autumn colors right.
No, we didn't know I'd be the one to stand alone,
smile at the goldfinch still yellow at the feeder,
wave at a cardinal's flashing red in the birch.
I'd be the one who'd get to say ... "Yes, yes."

THE HOSPITAL ROOM

They're laundering sheets
on the floor below
jarring the room
and my bed.
In the hall, a polisher hums,
hollow calls drone
on the intercom.
The door is closed.
On the window sill, a plant
with white frizzled blossoms,
a yellow ribbon.

Rick phoned from the west,
in *prime time,* said he loves it there.
Sees a mountain peak from his desk,
walks to tidepools only blocks away.

The nurse here, so young,
so anxious, wants me to know
she likes my plant,
that she closed my door.
She would encourage me, she says.
A student still, she gets A's, I'm sure.

I soak in this nothing to do,
nothing to think about,
to care about,
each moment a getting ready,
each day a leaving behind.

Rick, son, find me a place,
a soft earth place
where we can sit together
and mark the lives we dream of.
You take the big knotty limb
and running from corner to corner
carve your limits,
broad ones, deep ones.
I'll scratch the little twig tracks,
the tiny bird marks.
All I want. All I need.

AFTER THE TRIP TO THE DOCTOR

You are old, the voice said,
of course you are tired.
It's the leaves turning,
it's the morning chill.

Back on your porch, you doze,
no longer seeing the crows
crowd in the cottonwood,
or the last ducks spread
across the glossy lake.

Now you walk beside a stream
as blue as the sky.
How light the canoe across your shoulders,
how easily it slides off and into the water,
water that moves without splash or sound,
no ripples, no wake.
You flow over falls, then another falls,
then another.

You hold out your hat, a hat
you didn't know you owned,
now a wide dish.
Into the dish, the white moon drops,
already changing color.
Oh, no, the moon's not yours!
Quickly you lift it, how light it is,
and set it out on the water,
marveling as it begins to grow
and grow.

And your eyes close
until, at last, the glow encompasses
the river, the canoe and you.

STAYING BEHIND AT THE BED AND
BREAKFAST

Tip open again that tiny octagonal window
with its leaded panes and ancient paint
and watch them go.

Tip it open gently and watch them leave,
waving gloved hands at whizzing cabs.
Betty in her floppy traveler's hat,
Amy and Lynn with Irish flags and penny whistles
bulging from their shoulder bags,
off for a night of Irish pubs.

And you, three stories up, look down on a garden
where roses bloom in two straight rows
with a wide neat path between,
and the narrow gate is locked to the street.

Tip open again that tiny window.
Dusk now and lights appear.
Watch the cab pull to the curb,
accept their flouncing skirts,
and see them gone.

Feel again that drinking glass
warm with tap water coffee.
Savor the crumbling roll.
See the iron bed, the faded carpet.
hear those pages turning,
the lamp's soft click.

FACES

Life is an old bone even the dog has tired of,
a round bone he couldn't bite,
one that remains forever uncracked,
the marrow hidden.

With no trimmings, my love for you:
warm earth, no weeds there, no flowers either,
just the heat of the sun
and your body pressed on mine.

With no trimmings, my life
drawing to an end, the sky closer,
stars at eye level now,
the moon at arm's reach,
waiting for a touch, my touch.

Your face, my face, all the faces,
pure and plain. Here and now.

COMING HOME

It's time for all you heroes to come home,
time to hang the armor in the barn,
toss the crossbow in the woodpile,
time to sit by the fire, nursing the sores
on your feet. Give them a rest, on a
pillow, maybe, or in a pail of warm suds.

Is there no one there
who'll pat dry, gently? No? Then, you,
old hero, retired hero, tired hero,
you pat the feet, daub them with oil,
tuck them into warm wool. Heroes, too,
they've come a long road, filled with ruts and stones,
little stones that worked their way
into the shoes, the socks. Yes, it's time
for all you heroes to come home and shout
"Hey, we've done it."
The medals, the ribbons don't seem right anymore,
and off comes your jacket
with the epaulets and all the brass,
and how surprised you are. Who's that in the mirror?
Under that old skin, blotched and sagging,
is there someone . . . someone you never had time to know?
Well? "Hey, hello! how good, at last, to meet!"

AFTER DAYS OF BROODING ON INFINITY

Slow as a tortoise and weary
of the sawdust ring, you snore—
then sniff the grasses
and bound out of your stupor.
Life's a-wasting. Run, run!

Toss the fencepole across the hedgerow,
find the peacock and pull its feathers.
Smile and wail in one long screech,
then throw yourself upon the dog
and beg to be blessed.

Somewhere there's a dandy
in a top hat and jodhpurs,
shouting, "Save me! Save me!"
Forget the dandy! Find the pond
and blow your frosty breath upon it.

Watch it curl with watercress,
then fuming, push you toward
the light fantastic where you trip
until the morning after
when the cherry blossoms pluck you up

and lift you proudly to the sun,
"Take this wise one,
at last, oh, Master, and keep her
now forever after
in the whitest, purest alabaster."

THE SWING AT THE CABIN

Yesterday when the sky was bright
and our grandchildren rode bikes in the gravel
and the man who's our son climbed high in the trees
to fix me a swing, I was ready.

I caught his arm as he touched the ground,
said the words aloud:
All of life's a gift, even the pain,
remember that when I am gone.

Hug me again, the son said
after he roped the bikes to his car
and ordered his children in.
Then the car was gone, the dust settled.
Even the leaves were still.

I sat in the swing he'd made,
smelling of pine boards,
thought of his broad hands
you and I fashioned somehow
almost forty years ago.
I pumped the swing, flew high
over alders and tiny balsam,
heard the water on the rocks below.

Today I wake slowly, rain on the roof.
My head churns. I can't move
from bed to chair without a lurch.
Under the dripping trees, the swing
hangs limp. And you, you're not anywhere.

THE WAY IT IS

(after reading T. S. Eliot)

Nineteen ninety-seven. Already!
Very cold, the sun shines.
Too bright. And I, I am afraid.
Under the blankets, stretched out on my back.
This is what it will be like.
Just read "Prufrock." So beautiful, so sad.
"And in short, I was afraid."
Arthur came yesterday. The long talk.
Man, the incessant warrior,
forever battling, destroying . . .
and so it's ever been, Arthur said,
I no longer think there is a God.
And in short, *he* was afraid.
Long since I thought of that god in the sky,
the One who watches the sparrows fall.
Long since I cared. But I said nothing.
When Arthur left, the warm hug.
I'll always remember this, he said.
But son, what if? Oh, Arthur, don't leave . . .
The cold! The cold!
My wrist hurts, my arm feels unattached.
Hey, Arm, re-attach! Commands.
Learn to give commands: Boy, shovel my walk.
Bring me the mail, bring me coffee, bring me
a new arm, a new leg.
Carnations, there in the window,
let me be your daughter,
fragrant, white, prim in a glass vase.
I do not think I want the quiet broken.

I do not think I want to dream. All those expectations . . .
Let us stop then, you and I,
and praise all that is good below and above.
Soon enough the bed at the end of the hall, the long hall.
The rose in the hand.
Soon enough the night and no dawn at all.

ON RE-READING GREAT POEMS

Yesterday and the day before,
I could fathom easily their depths,
scale easily the heights they rose to.
Brave words—carrying me
to the greatest of days, of hours.
Today the same words rust
about my moistened lips, striking no sparks.

And what of that? The lake is here,
still as it's ever been; an odor of decaying fish
rises in the breeze. Now and then,
through the underbrush and tall trees,
a child's voice, the rumble of cars on the highway.

Perhaps this is a day to note the fog
on the rim of the distant bay, the pinkish shade
of the water a mile up the shore.
"What a lovely view you have."
Not a view but a place, my place.

SELF PORTRAIT

The sun shines through a gate of a cloister,
leaves a pattern on the floor of the dark hall.
She wants in there,
she's always wanted the quiet place,
the walled-in space, the only sounds,
the clang of an iron gate, the swish
of long black skirts in the garden.

But she's not in a garden, she's in a beehive:
a drone, buzzing, working, moving. In and out,
above and below, never, never stopping.

About the Author

This is the first book-length collection of poetry by Lucille Broderson, 94, who began writing poems when she joined her husband, Phil, in a poetry class they took in their early 60s.

Two chapbooks, *A Thousand Years* (Pudding House Publications) and *Beware* (Spout Press), were published in 2002. Individual poems have appeared in *Poetry, Tri-Quarterly, Nimrod, Agassiz Review* and *Ironwood*, as well as in several anthologies, including *Thirty-three Minnesota Poets* and *The Wind Blows, the Ice Breaks: Poems of Loss and Renewal by Minnesota Poets,* both published by Nodin Press.

Lucille has won the Loft Mentor competition, the Lake Superior Regional Writers Competition, was twice a finalist in the "Discovery"/*The Nation* poetry contest, and has received a Minnesota State Arts Board grant. Garrison Keillor has read her poems on *The Writer's Almanac*.

She would like to express her gratitude to the people "who said she could write poetry": Andrew Hudgins, Jim Moore, Patricia Hampl and Michael Dennis Browne. And she especially wants to thank her daughter-in-law, Linda Close Broderson.